Through Your Troubles To The Stars

Here it is, for all those out there,
in their hardest of times, putting their
heart and soul into something. It's taken my lifetime
to finally get to the stage where I have begun
to openly share the fact that I am a scribbler
of sentiments (I still struggle with the word poet).
I hid it, through embarrassment and a
lack of confidence for years and thought
it to be silly and somewhat non sensical. Yet
still at the same time, I always had this ambition
inside of me, to one day, be able to say
that I have written a book.
The content may well not be to everyones
liking, and this may never adorn the bookshelves
of many.
But...
I have now written a book, and whoever you are,
you are about to read at least some of it.

One ambition now realised
and I thank you.
Sincerely.

Ryan Cuthbert

aka

Mesentire

Contents

1. Acapella Heart
2. Reading Her
3. So Close
4. Soul Dancer
5. So Long Sorrow
6. The Eye
7. Shamed Stars
8. But
9. Dream Catcher
10. For Keeps
11. Testing The Waters
12. Time
13. Star Shimmer
14. Drifting
15. Scars
16. Speechless
17. Mute Heart
18. Taken
19. The Journey
20. First Sight
21. I See
22. Happy Heart
23. Just Enough
24. Herself
25. Nothing
26. Follow
27. The Spaces

28. Irony
29. Promises & Wishes
30. Better Days
31. The Rain
32. The Shadow
33. Wine
34. Leave
35. Together
36. Misunderstood
37. You Know Who
38. Eyes Wide Open
39. My Place
40. Paying Attention
41. Magic From Mayhem
42. Sweet & Sour
43. Sometimes
44. The End
45. The Storm
46. Unwritten
47. Held
48. Graced
49. A Vision
50. Selfish
51. Brush Strokes
52. Somebody
53. Freedom
54. Changing Seasons
55. Fake Smiles
56. Balance

57. Madness
58. Not Looking
59. Value
60. Doors
61. She
62. Mistake
63. You
64. ?
65. What If
66. Eyes Wide Shut
67. Thoughts
68. Self Destruct
69. She Was There
70. True Love
71. Turn Around
72. My Midnight
73. The Great Unknown
74. Calamity
75. A Walk
76. Direction
77. Looking
78. Blind
79. Strong
80. How
81. Tunnel
82. Puzzle
83. Haunt
84. Fear Of The Fall
85. Compelled

86. Fell In Love With A Poet
87. A Dreamers Promise
88. Warmth
89. Your Truth
90. The Guide
91. Lucky
92. Morning Beautiful
93. The Girl Who Cried
94. The Fantasy
95. Spellbound
96. Pssst
97. Stardust
98. Ironic
99. Ad Astra
100. Listening
101. Re Reading
102. Catching Stars
103. There
104. Another
105. Shadows
106. Tell Her
107. Undeniable
108. No Luck
109. Acceptance
110. Lost & Found
111. My Education
112. Fingertips
113. Hidden
114. Puddles

115. Holding
116. Shards
117. The Mystery
118. The Knowing
119. Firsts
120. The One
121. Whispers
122. That Smile You Wear
123. Romance
124. Sighs
125. Why
126. Clarity
127. Flames
128. Beauty
129. Undressed
130. Cry
131. The Storm
132. Remedy
133. Sunburn
134. Daydream
135. Failing
136. Simple Things
137. Just Me
138. The Hunger
139. Masterpiece
140. Home

Through Your Troubles To The Stars

A CAPELLA HEART

In pursuit of fantasy
finding something real
emotions resurrected
learn once again to feel
the rhythm of a heart
that beats in unison with mine
to find her simply follow
my stars above that shine
she is music, she is melody
she is poetry and art
and my soul can't help but dance
to her a capella heart

READING HER

She seems to some, no more
than a closed book, and I
just continue to read.
While occasionally skipping back
to the corners I left folded,
on the pages of my favourite
chapters, never wanting to reach
"The End"

SO CLOSE

I simply wish to be
so close to you
that I can taste your breath
as I am taking it away

SOUL DANCER

She dances through the storms
turns nightmare into daydream
she brings serenity and calm
as chaos reigns supreme
she stops the world from crashing
for those whose hearts she holds to tight
and she lights up all the shadows
like the stars that chase the night
she is wonder, she is awe
she is beauty, giver, lover
she is friend and she is soul mate
she is daughter, she is mother
taking nothing for herself
no single second in a day
and I wish that I could stop time
to only make her stay

SO LONG, SORROW

I was a little in love with sorrow
learned to live along with pain
and though the sun fell through my window
I missed dancing in the rain
those memories bring misery
yet a smile can keep me sane
I had you, and I held you
now my heart beats once again

THE EYE

There's a
hurricane
blowing
through my
heart
and your
smile is
the eye
of the
storm

SHAMED STARS

Even the
memory
of her
kiss
burns so
brightly
that the
stars are
put
to
shame

BUT

what if you
are not mine
and I
am not yours

and what if
we are
not destined
to occupy
the same
space
forever

what if this
isn't
all that
it seems

oh but...

what if it is

DREAM CATCHER

and
all I
want
to do
is make
her dreams
come
true

FOR KEEPS

when she tells you
all you've wanted to hear

listen to her

when she shows you
all you've wanted to see

look at her

when she stirs in you
all the emotions you wished to feel

love her

when she gives to you
all you've wanted to hold

take her

and when you've found
the one you were seeking all along

keep her

TESTING THE WATERS

Do not
dip a toe
into the
waters
if you
are not
ready
to get
swept away
by the
current

TIME

His expressionless face
and hard hitting hands
keeping you from me
offering you second hand love
as he runs out on you again

oh how I wish

to stop him dead
turn him back
move him along
but I cannot fight him

he is time

and he refuses to stand still

STARS SHIMMER

Oh soul mirror
hopes glimmer
bonded by a stars shimmer

a loves suppose
lost in the throes
of two hearts beating
in unified echoes

wanting, needing, hiding
searching, seeking, finding

I for her, she for me
finally, the eyes can see
first sight, yet a recognise
a dawning of true loves sunrise
twin flames reflection within her eyes

a dream remains though now awoken
hearing words left once unspoken
both existed as they meet
together, one,
two halves complete

DRIFTING

it wasn't
that I'd
searched
for her

more that
we'd let go
of all that
weighed
us down
and
then we
simply drifted
towards
one
another

SCARS

She healed my scars
in such a way
that it was worth
being wounded
after all

SPEECHLESS

I loved the
sound of
her voice
and
yet
my heart fills
with her
silence
when I say those words
that render her speechless

MUTE HEART

Protecting your
heart is like
keeping a bird
caged
and forever
wondering
just why
it won't
sing

TAKEN

She
takes
me
to
a
place
that
makes
me
forget
there's
anywhere
else

THE JOURNEY

and she became
the only journey
in which I had
no desire
to ever reach
my destination

FIRST SIGHT

Love at first sight:

the very
moment
that the
heart
recognises
just what
the soul
has been
searching for

I SEE

With my eyes closed
I see the shape of her
watch her
moving
arching
writhing
I hear her, taste her, feel her,
beneath me
beside me
above me
enveloping me
replaying every scene
every minute
every second
the memory of her, a reality
yet the thought of her
still my fantasy

HAPPY HEART

a
happy
heart
cannot
have
it's
head
turned

JUST ENOUGH

Some days it's just too much
to have too little, I speak in sighs
some nights I'm with you, while without you
and to see you, close my eyes
there's times my hand is holding
on to thoughts of how you feel
and my imagination questions
while you're gone, if you were real
my empty heart, beats full of you
and I'm seeking you to find
your voice whispering my name
just in the echoes of my mind
I reminisce as I am missing
I wear your smile upon my face
my "without you" times, tick slowly
when I'm with you seconds race
my busy head is doubt free though
assured in knowing I'm in love
and too much, of those too little times
it seems, are just enough

HERSELF

She looks
into a mirror
and she sees
only "herself"
though the rest
of the world
becomes blinded
by the brightness
of her
reflection

NOTHING

The
nothing
that
she
sees
in
herself
is
everything
to
me

FOLLOW

Follow where it leads
listen when it speaks
for though it suffered breakage
the heart still knows what it seeks

THE SPACES

I can't say
if what you're
feeling
is right
or if
it is wrong
but you're feeling
and those feelings
made their way in
because
there was space
for them
to

your issues
are not the feelings
your issues
are
the spaces

IRONY

The beautiful irony
when your heart
pains in the absence
of another
yet you know
that feels better
than the emptiness
before they
filled it

PROMISES	WISHES
It's the	It's the
sharp	unbreakable
edges	bond
of a	of a
broken	selfless
promise	wish
that	that
cuts a	holds
heart	the pieces
into	back in
two	place

BETTER DAYS

The sun is shining
right before you
new horizons
better days

reflections
from the water
your thoughts
lost in the haze

shows a picture
of bright futures
it paints
with golden rays

THE RAIN

Listen to
the rain
drumming his fingers
the sound
of my impatience
waiting
to see you
again

THE SHADOW

I'm
head over heels
and
my world
is bright as
a result

who knew
the darkness
was simply
a shadow
cast by
a heavy heart

WINE

Hearing her
sentiments
whispered in my ear
just as sweet
as the taste
of wine
from her lips

LEAVE

when
somebody
on
the
outside
makes
you
question
what's
on
the
inside

it's
time
to
close
the
door

TOGETHER

To become
more together
first you must
let go
of those
that made
you fall
apart

MISUNDERSTOOD

I spoke silently out loud
repeating every unused word
focussed not, on what I didn't say
I failed to watch what wasn't heard

I misinterpreted wrongly
the closed eyed looks I didn't see
incorrectly misunderstanding
the complex simplicity of me

YOU KNOW WHO

There exists a person
and you'll always remember
just where and just when you met
and remember all that was said
you'll always remember
the sound of their laughter
and just how their eyes light up as they smile
that person will trigger a thousand memories
as they flash across your mind
for a second
and you'll remember forever
the way your heart fills
when they speak your name
there exists a person
and you'll always remember
just how
whenever you're with them
you can just forget
everything else

EYES WIDE OPEN

Staying awake
was favoured
above the love of sleep
in fear of
not dreaming
of each other each night

MY PLACE

There's a secret place we go to
when we run away from all
a place we go to sit
when we're failing to stand tall
there's a somewhere that saves us
when the sadness makes us ache
and that place to hide a heart away
knowing it won't break
there's a place that during grey skies
clouds break and sun shines through
where storms exist only
to fuel the rainbows hue
there's a place I often hideaway
in tough times and when I'm blue
there's a secret place we go to
and my place my dear is you

PAYING ATTENTION

If you see past
the smile
and you hear
beyond the words
you'll find
lost
within the beauty
of her soul
the pain of where
her broken heart
still weeps

MAGIC FROM MAYHEM

In the quiet of the night
I find myself believing
once again
in magic
and in the coming true of dreams
as morning fog begins to descend
making halos from each star
before the sun is ready to rise
I feel an angel
peering down on me
amid the constellations
and laying my demons to rest
in graves
that soon shall be home
to flowers
of hope in bloom

SWEET AND SOUR

It isn't always
necessary to
whisper those
sweet nothings

no

come shout
your sour
somethings
to me too

SOMETIMES

Sometimes
I say your
name
so that
you're once again
upon my lips
when the
taste of your kiss
has faded

THE END

Just as I
was ready
to face
the end

she
holds me
like a new
beginning

THE STORM

It wasn't
that she had learned
to dance
through the storms
but more that she knew
that there
dancing
within her heart
a storm would grow
tossing aside the debris of old loves
so new love
could take root
in the eye

UNWRITTEN

Words
on
paper
still
do
not
compare
to
all
that's
left
unwritten

HELD

Even when
I can't hold you
I still won't
let you go

GRACED

She'll walk in
like an
unassuming
Angel
never knowing
the effect
on all others
graced
by her presence

A VISION

To see her
but for a moment
is to hold
the memory of her
for
a lifetime

SELFISH

My most
selfish thought
is that if
I had the power
to stop the world from turning
I'd do it
simply so that
time with you
wouldn't pass

BRUSH STROKES

Each kiss
a brush stroke
painting pictures
of you
upon my
canvas heart

SOMEBODY

To become a somebody
you simply have
to step away
from everybody
that think's that you
are a nobody

FREEDOM

Freedom:

understanding
that it's not selfish
to want something
that you consider
enough

CHANGING SEASONS

Come out of the cold
out of hibernation
a changing of
emotional seasons
is upon you
begin your Spring time
feast after famine
fill your hungry heart
and enjoy all of the warmth
that Summer can bring
before you Fall again

FAKE SMILES

We deny ourselves
the chances
to chase
further happiness
as we gift those
closest to us
with the
fake versions
of our
smiles

BALANCE

Take
from
each
person
less
than
you
give

and
you'll
always
leave
with
more

MADNESS

To talk to yourself
is madness
to write to yourself
is poetry

NOT LOOKING

Some people
spend a
lifetime
looking for something
and finding
nothing
the lucky ones
are not looking
for anything
and yet
find something
incredible

VALUE

Whoever you may be
you think
you're not worth it?
there's somebody
out there
right now
thinking you're worth
so much more

DOORS

They'll walk into
your life
those special ones
not by opening
a door
but first
by opening
your eyes

SHE

She touches hearts
she sees inside of people
and then
shows to them
just what that looks like
she
is beautiful
in so many ways
but that
is the most beautiful
way of all

MISTAKE

If this
isn't
meant to be
then it
is simply
the greatest
mistake
I have ever
made

YOU

Words
escape
me
as
my
mind
is
full
of
you

?

I can
no more
explain
the stars
than I can
understand
this
love

WHAT IF

All of my
"what ifs"
each of my
"if onlys"
exist within
the heart
that beats
inside of
her chest

EYES WIDE SHUT

I close my eyes
on tougher days
and
drift
away
to that place
where first I saw
your smile

THOUGHTS

There's a thought I have
a thought I get lost in
a thought that makes me smile
stirs within me
a happiness I've never before encountered
soothes me
exhilarates me
brings me both desire and satisfaction
a thought that drives me wild
and yet calms me
both at once
there's a thought I have
that makes me become
the very best of me
makes me believe in dreams
in wishes
in magic
makes me feel enough
there's a thought I have
and that thought
is always
just of you

SELF DESTRUCT

I was never taught
the difference between
self-preservation
and self-destruct
and I fought
once again
with my demons
while my angel overlooked

SHE WAS THERE

She was there
the whole time
my lowest time
breaking my fall
never letting me hit the floor
she was there
building me up
putting me back together
piece by piece
she was there
and with her two arms
and warming heart
she'd hold me closer
just when I was falling apart
she was there
as I then fell in love
with the one
that accompanied me
in my darkness
and I wonder if
she'll ever really know
just how much light
she brings

TRUE LOVE

True love is the
expression of emotion
felt through the
rhythm of a heart
that makes the soul
of another
dance in time

TURNAROUND

There'll be days when you
feel afraid to walk towards
the future
that you've been heading for
turn then instead
to the past
that you've been moving away from
and you'll soon
pick up the pace again

MY MIDNIGHT

When I became empty
lost
a vacant desolation
of who I once was
when the light within me
was no more
than a smouldering ember
she still loved
the spaces in between
and stepped into
my midnight
to do just that

THE GREAT UNKNOWN

I am not the thunder
I am the silence in between
I am not the stars that shine
but the night that keeps them seen
I am not torrential rain
I am the earth that soaks away
I am not the break of dawn
but the moon that fades for day
I am not the ocean
I am the stream that fills the sea
I am not the free birds flight
but nesting branches of the tree
I am not the candle light
I am the match that burned the wick
I am not the time that flies
but the hands that make it tick
I am not the beauty seen
I am the mirror held before
I am not the tidal wave
but the sand that waits ashore
I am not the standing crowd
I am the company of alone
I am not invisible
but I am the great unknown

CALAMITY

I have been a calamity
at the bottom of bottles
that I've held with greasy fingers
that smell of stale cigarettes.
lost in meaningless conversations
with bar room nobodies,
taking strangers as friends
in the absence of real connection.
I've ran from the four walls
that house mirrors
which reveal a reflection
that I need to escape.
I've walked from glass to glass to glass,
refills taking preference to
cab rides home.
I am the pretender that wears the smile
of contentment and confidence,
keeping only my lonely shadow
close enough to sleep with.
I battle my mind to be still,
as it taunts me with with dreams my
fingers cannot hold.
my wishes just to exist, sink as another drink
is poured, and I stare at my phone,
just wanting to read the text that says
"come to me, I am yours now"

A WALK

Some days
I find myself
going for
little walks
through every
thought of you
I've ever had

DIRECTION

There'll be times when you don't know
where you're going
or even in which direction you're headed
times you've no clue if you've taken
a wrong turn or if the path
is worth even one more step
it's going to be tough
you're going to stumble
perhaps even a fall or two
you'll feel pain and yes you'll cry
but you'll get there, you'll get there
and when you do you'll know
that each falter was a lesson
each moment you saw as weakness
was actually building strength
each doubt was merely guidance
you'll get there
and you'll turn and remember
mainly the smiles
and the sunshine and the laughter
and the friends you made along the way
you'll be exactly where you need to be
exactly when you need to be there
welcome to your journey you beautiful soul
and be assured that your destination
will be worth every second of it

LOOKING

She doesn't hide from me
and yet
I find her
in all of the places
I look

BLIND

Though she saw
the love
in all she laid
her eyes upon
still she fails
to see
the beauty
in herself

STRONG

Don't feel weak because
somebody chose to break you
feel strong
that you gave enough
to stretch you to the point of fragility
don't allow them to change
the beauty of the person within
remember
you
are somebodies "enough"
they are just waiting
for you to turn up

HOW

When the eyes no longer see
and the ears hear only silence
when the hands can not quite reach
and the mouths dare not speak
when the paper has all been burned
and the ink has run dry
how then
do you tell them
that they're loved?

TUNNEL

Love her
so deeply
that it can
tunnel beneath
and leave her walls
intact

PUZZLE

You may see your pieces
as a broken mess
but
to somebody
you are a beautiful
puzzle
to solve

HAUNT

The solitude
that entertains
your days
can haunt you
in the
night

FEAR OF THE FALL

On the days you
can no longer hold on
the bravest move
is to just
let
go
loosen your grip
the drop
is kinder
than the fear
of
the
fall

COMPELLED

When there can be no other
than to follow
compulsion
that is when you know
nature guides you
to what
will be

FELL IN LOVE WITH A POET

He spent his life hidden
an unknown to all he
interacts with, choosing to
only let them see the mask
that they wished to see.
then she walked into his world
and with each intoxicating
interlaced word, she painted
pictures of him, in the colours
of her love. and there for his
first time, he saw himself through
eyes that loved him, and began to
learn himself again.
coincidence had struck and fate
had played a guiding hand as
these two stars collided.
he'd fallen in love with a poet,
and she'd written away his mask.

A DREAMERS PROMISE

I told you all my secrets
and I shared with you my fears
I kept you just far enough
that you couldn't see the tears

I held your hand and told you
that I have failed on the way
and I may not be the best for you
so you don't have to stay

and there in that very moment
through tears of your own
you held my hand close to your chest
and told me I was home

and I say things you can't hear
as I watch you while you sleep
dream filled whispers from my lips
of every promise that I'll keep

WARMTH

I am so deeply full of you
I want to hold you
while you lay with me
and bring you a warmth
that makes your heart feel
like forever isn't long enough

YOUR TRUTH

You'll find your truth in an honest heart
and the voice you long to hear
will balance an unsteady soul
and doubt will disappear

THE GUIDE

She is not the light
at the end of the tunnel
she is the hand
that guides me
through the dark

LUCKY

Drowning in uncertain times
with darkened realities looming
over an ever nearing horizon
one hand one my shoulder
three words in my ear
and then there
as she said
the sun rises to greet us
and tomorrow is faced with a roar
as I was prepared to fall
to falter
to disappear into the shadow
she points me towards the light
takes me by the hand
and pulls me into the unknown
the unfamiliar
the new
she takes me to the place
where "alone" does not exist
and I ask myself simply
"how did I get so lucky?"

MORNING BEAUTIFUL

the sun,   she rises
a sign to   my heart
that it's now time
to fall in love
with you
again
x

THE GIRL WHO CRIED

He wiped away her tears
and told her the world
was actually a wonderful place
and she believed him
because he was in it

THE FANTASY

My thoughts drift
and my imagination
compels me to explore
notions of just how
wonderful it must feel
to wake up next to you
and have nothing in
my mind but thoughts
of last night

SPELLBOUND

I don't know if
it's how her voice
enchants me
how her smile
has me captivated
how her eyes draw
me into an imaginary world
where no other exists
if it's how her touch
reminds me I'm alive
if it's the sight of her
sound of her
feel of her
I don't know if it's the fact
she's reality and fantasy
each at the same time
I don't know just what it is
there's something about that girl
it's magic
and I am spellbound

PSSST

It turns out
that feeling empty
is just your heart
making enough space
to be filled
by the next one
to love you

STARDUST

I know the world is dark
some days, and I know the
path is hard, but you have
enough light inside of you,
to guide you around the
stones on your path. shine
on, and cast your shadows
behind you, over all you
wish to forget. shine on,
for your soul is made
of stardust, and the dark
is afraid of you.

IRONIC

The ironic thing is
that with every
breath you take away
I feel more alive

AD ASTRA

I traced the marks
upon her skin
and
drew a pathway
to my stars

LISTENING

and it's only
the truly
beautiful
amongst us
that begin
to listen
once all
the words
run out

RE-READING

You're my favourite
book to read
and I've turned back
all your corners
torn the cover
and left coffee rings
on some pages
yet still when I pick you up
I don't know how
you're going
to end

CATCHING STARS

Love is as rare as stardust
there are no rules
no hard and fast guidelines
that tell us how to feel
when to act
or
who to fall for
there will come times of adoration
affection, infatuation
there will come times of emptiness
neglect and rejection
life moves in cycles
ride the storm
until the sun shines again
learn to let go when nobody
else is still holding on
and that will leave your grip ready
to catch the next
star that falls

THERE

There
right there
that spot
where your shoulder
meets your neck
that
right there
is where my lips
call home

ANOTHER

You are
the shot
at the bar
that once
tasted I
feel an
undeniable
urge
to order
another

SHADOWS

Once they shed
a little light
on themselves
you can learn
to love
their shadows too

TELL HER

She may
already know
but look
into her eyes
hold her
let her feel
the desire
the urges
and the necessity
of having her
and tell her

like you mean it

UNDENIABLE

You can't stop it,
nor can you force it.
controlling it is not
an option you can take.
you're not driving it,
but neither are you just
along for the ride.
my love, the magnitude of
emotion overwhelms you,
I know, and equally at times
leaves you empty in the absences.
this is what you were born
to find, and it has found you.
rationality and logic rule you,
and yet you feel your senses have
abandoned you, and your mind
has lost all focus. your heart beats
with a passion, right out
of your chest, and in an instant
can become too heavy to carry,
while the soul that has always felt
content, suddenly feels like it has been
missing this your whole life.
be both excited and afraid, because you
have fallen in love, and there's
no turning back from here

NO LUCK

There is no luck
only being open to see
and to grab whatever
life desires to offer you
you've always got the
same two choices
take it
or leave it
that is not luck
that is you
being the pilot
of your destiny

ACCEPTANCE

Accepting that there's
nothing more
that you can do
isn't giving up
it's
moving on

LOST AND FOUND

I find myself
so far away
from who
I've been
that I'm almost
who I am
again

MY EDUCATION

Learning her
is so much fun
that I hope to
never
fully
know her

FINGERTIPS

She
writes her
next chapter
in the palm of
my hand
with her fingertip
and I pray
she never writes
the end

HIDDEN

some days I awake, and the world becomes so heavy, that it sits upon my chest, making me unable to breathe. I've shown the world my smiles, when my eyes are really sparkling because one more blink, and I'll cry. My laughter has been heard, though being forced past the lump in my throat. I express love easily, and even with my broken pieces, I'll try to fix someone, anyone, everyone, first. Somehow people see confidence, they see courage, they see strength and they see me, just as I wish them to. But I hurt, I fucking hurt so badly. I've been let down, denied, forgotten about. I've been cheated, demoralised and devalued. I see no worth in myself at times.
I see no reason in my existence. I gave everything I had, and everything I was to an empty chasm that took from me even more still. I am so empty of ego, that I'm inside fucking out. All I ever did, was be the me that others wished for me to be. I didn't falter, I didn't fail, I lived up to every expectation. I played by the rules. I am he, protector, provider, lover, father, hunter, gatherer. I am a man that was needed in so many ways, but never wanted in any. I am alone in crowds. I am still smiling, you'll still hear my laughter, and from the world, I will remain hidden.

PUDDLES

I once thought
of love
as a raindrop
and I'd jump in
the puddles as
it fell
then she showed me
it was a torrent
and I've been
drowning
in her ocean
ever since

HOLDING

Though I hold
her heart
in my hands
I find myself
still trying to
steal it
each day
that I wake

SHARDS

He was not all he seemed
lost inside the shadows of
his own demons
outwardly giving to every
heart he touched
but silently he wept for somebody
to notice that he was in pieces
hoping there was a soul to match
his own
who'd put him back together
oh
but when she came
she offered no repair
she simply held all the shards in
her gentle hands
shining her love onto them
and filling his world
with a light and a beauty
that could never have existed
without first being
beautifully broken

THE MYSTERY

He couldn't quite
put his finger on it
but
having seen it
in her eyes
he was prepared
to spend a lifetime
finding out
just what it was

THE KNOWING

There is a depth here
when I feel her
see her
eye to eye with her
no words are necessary
no effort needed
just the knowing is enough
she inspires me
she impresses me
she attracts me
and she really makes me like myself
because I know that she sees me
and that I'm enough to make her smile
I find myself loving her
and I'm realising that up until now
I don't think I've ever
been loved back

FIRSTS

First sight
first touch
first kiss
I wish
to turn back
to only have
those firsts
once more.
that night
chasing down the sun
holding onto the moon
trying to evade dawn
the crashing waves
the soundtrack to
the fact time was passing
sunrise
marked the demise
of an ending
of those firsts
now I wish
to turn back time
to have those firsts
once more

THE ONE

She's the pre- cursor
she's the prologue
she's the conclusion
she's the epitaph
she's my before
she's my after
she's my during
and though my heart can bleed
I know she catches every drop
and when I breathe out all the air
that my lungs can hold
before I suffocate
she puts her lips to mine
and breathes life back
into the void

WHISPERS

Oh there is was all along
reflected in a teardrop
and in the words of every song
and though the walls they have been building
and the doors are closing to the light
as the shimmer of a dream fades
and hope gets lost inside the night
but a heart can't do the choosing
and a head can't learn to feel
fingers can't hold onto
what imagination knows is real
the answer in her words
and the truth within her eyes
from exasperated questions
asked by my soulful sighs
and just when I had let go
final brick up on my wall
descending into darkness
she somehow stops my fall
with nothing more than whispers
from within her beating heart
she awakens, forsaken feelings
and takes me right back to the start

THAT SMILE YOU WEAR

Though you know
because you're often told
still it's needing to be said
that thoughts of you
that smile you wear
are present in my head
I once had me some alone time
now you join me in that place
because thoughts of you
that smile you wear
fill that lonely space
and it's something you're aware of
not some secret that I keep
that thoughts of you
that smile you wear
come to see me in my sleep
I give to you just all I can
and there's just one thing I'll take
a thought of you
that smile you wear
to be there when I wake

ROMANCE

The chasing
of what one dreams of
in the belief
that you can catch it
and create a perfect moment
by doing so
I believe I can catch you
and I know the moment
would be perfect
so yes
this is romance

SIGHS

you can measure
how much
you love a person
by how deeply
you sigh
when you're wishing
they were here

WHY?

She
was the kind
of wonderful
that when you
told her so
her reply
was simply
why?

CLARITY

She'll come
when you expect her least
and open up your eyes
though you'd no idea
you'd even been asleep
she'll shine her light
into your life
veiled darkness falls away
she's casting shadows out
that you never knew were in you
she brings clarity and depth
and self-conscious reawakening
yet her gifts
are what you never knew you needed
she is beauty
she is fire
the object of affection
she's necessity
she's desire
she is you
and she
is love

FLAMES

Intense thoughts
of steamy sheets
breathlessness
and pounding beats
of hearts that burst
almost too much
for bodies weakened
by lovers' touch
exploring each
with fingertips
as hungry mouth
meets trembling lips
the fires burn
with passion bright
and my soul smoulders
from flames of last night

BEAUTY

Her beauty is her love
and she gave it
without asking
a thing in return
it grew within me
so strongly
roots took hold
and enabled me
to love again
now I have it
I will give it
without asking a thing in return
to her

UNDRESSED

Let's not dress
this up with
words of love
and let's leave
romance on
the floor
like discarded
underwear
while I lose
my eloquence
and let my
vocabulary
rest awhile
instead
let me hear
the language of
your body crying
out for all
of the talk
that mine
is ready
to say

CRY

The truth is
sometimes
you have to let
a little cry
out
to let a little
smile
in

THE STORM

Do you know
the majesty of a storm
in all its glory
can captivate me
and halt me in my tracks
no matter where I'm going
both bewildered and enchanted
equally
lost in that moment
held
transfixed
but a storm
in all it's majestic glory
stands not a chance
to steer away my focus
once my eyes
are locked
onto those
of your own

JUST ME

That was all she was, she said
he didn't see the same
she thought herself, nothing special
but he? he liked this game
he now got to tell her openly
all the things he saw
the obvious physical beauty
but, his seeing, saw, much more
he saw innocence, and impishness
he saw strength, and weakness too
his watchful eye paid attention
so the list of his seeings grew
he'd noticed care and compassion
wit and wisdom, pain, but just
such an unjudgmental nature
that still filled her world with trust
he'd seen maternal instinct
and also fire deep within
he'd spotted her angelic ways
and seen the presence of some sin
he told her all he'd seen in her
and he made her believe that he'd see
that the wonderful person before him
would always be more than "just me"

REMEDY

It seems a heart must break
before it finds the love
it deserves
just as dark comes before dawn
and rain before shine
pain too, before remedy
where heartbreak is concerned
love is the cure
not the cause

SUNBURN

I spent so long
basking
in her light
that her soul
left my heart
a little
sunburned

DAYDREAM

She was beautiful
I was awake
she was the reason
still I chased her
like clinging to a dream
that vanishes
at dawn

FAILING

On the days I fail
to feel my best
she talks to me
in a way
that makes
me believe
that the best
is yet to come

SIMPLE THINGS

Then she asked of him

"do you really think that you can fix me"

his response was simply

"no"

"but I will show you that you're not broken"

THE HUNGER

Beyond the words
above the thoughts
past the feelings
there's a necessity
a need
a desire
an urgency
there's the hunger
that my very being
craves the essence
of all that you are
to hear you
smell you
taste you
touch you
to have you
my soul, simply put
is incomplete
without yours
and as true as my heart beats
I know
that you're the one
sent
to satisfy
my starving
soul

MASTERPIECE

Her words are so
artistic
that I wish to
frame each one
that falls
from her mouth
with
my lips

HOME

There's not always going
to be any rhyme nor reason
for the things you don't
understand
some things just are
don't waste your precious time
trying
to fathom the answers
to your questions
just accept
that when you hold her
and you feel
like you're home
it's just because
you are

A Few Thankyous, credits, and plugs.

For the design and production of the cover art, many thanks to Chris Wain, I love how it looks Chris, you're awesome. (Scan the code to link to his Facebook page and check out his artwork)

Just because I think he's a bit good, here's a shameless plug to Christopher Lloyd Quintons music page. I wish him success, so please visit and help widen his audience.

Thank you also, to the very few that I did share scribbles with over the years, and who had always told me to "do something with them". Two that are prominent are my "old" (not aged) teacher, Mrs. Barker, and Lisa Bale, who for some reason kept hold of many of my teenage attempts to write what was going on in my pinball head.

I can't not go into print, without a thank you to my best buddy, Shaun Hiles, he's seen the rise and fall, the dark and light, the laughter and tears, and pretty much been the closest I have to a brother in this world. Cheers mate.

You'll have noticed, there's some deep-rooted sentiment within these pages, and, I guess, I found a muse in a heart that is helping mine to heal. So I wish to thank her too. She knows who she is.

I have to say once more, thank you to anyone who has liked, followed, shared and commented, on my facebook page, and Instagram, you have helped the confidence, and self belief to grow a little to give me the courage to go for this, and thank you to anybody that has wasted their hard earned cash to be reading this now.

Through Your Troubles To The Stars

For the ones I may never get to share this with, I want to say
that I love and miss you, Josh and Kenz.
I will always hold onto hope. x

Printed in Great Britain
by Amazon